1 Men of the Royal Army Medical Corps. The soldier on the right has been used as an example of how to dress an arm wound correctly, *c.* 1898

2 General Sir Colin Campbell and his chief-of-staff Major-General William Mansfield hearing 'good news and dispatches', Indian Mutiny, 1857

The Victorian and Edwardian

ARMY

from old photographs

commentaries by

JOHN FABB

Introduction by

W. Y. CARMAN

FSA, FRHistS

(Ex-Deputy Director of the National
Army Museum, London)

B.T.BATSFORD LTD

LONDON and SYDNEY

Visual Studies Workshop
Research Center
Rochester, N.Y.

3.20.6

First published 1975
© Captions John Fabb; Introduction W. Y. Carman 1975
ISBN 0 7134 2973 9

Printed in Great Britain by
The Anchor Press, Tiptree, Essex
for the publishers B.T.Batsford Ltd,
4 Fitzhardinge Street, London W1H 0AH
and 23 Cross Street, Brookvale, NSW 2100 Australia

3 Pioneer sergeant H. Tesh of the
Coldstream Guards, 1896. The pioneers
march at the head of the regiment and are
allowed to grow beards

CONTENTS

ACKNOWLEDGMENTS

I would like to thank those many museums which kindly offered photographs which, for reasons of space, could not be used. Acknowledgment is gratefully given to those from which photographs have been used:

Aberdeen University Library 37

John Fabb 1, 3, 5, 10, 11, 13, 14, 16–30, 22–33, 36, 38–44, 46, 53, 112, 113, 115, 116, 124–6, 137, 139–147, 150–2, 154

By gracious permission of Her Majesty the Queen 6–9, 34, 35, 51, 76, 77, 84, 86, 87, 91, 92, 54–9, 65, 71, 74–7

Household Cavalry Museum, Windsor 15, 45, 47–50

India Office Library 69, 99–101, 109, 111, 138

Institute of the Royal Artillery, Woolwich 128–31

Kent County Archive 4, 114, 127

Mansell Collection 67

National Army Museum 2, 61–4, 66, 68, 70, 72–5, 78–83, 85, 88, 90, 93, 94–6, 98, 102–8, 110, 117–23, 133–6, 148

Victoria and Albert Museum 21, 60, 89, 97

Illustrations 149 and 153 are from the Publisher's collection.

Thanks are also due to Douglas Sellick of Batsford for his able assistance in the picture research.

4 Captain McGregor and his men of the 97th Regiment, 1855. A drummer stands on the left. The forage caps bear the regimental number

INTRODUCTION

For many years the life of the soldier could only be described in words or depicted by works of an artist who had his own techniques or ideas to limit his powers of expression. The early years of the nineteenth century saw the emergence of a new idea – that of showing a person exactly as he or she was. The production of shadow portraits or silhouettes had been one step in this direction. The use of the camera obscura could trap a living scene with people in a darkened room but the image was transient and disappeared. However efforts were being made to fix such an image. The slow development of the processes which we know today as photography gradually opened a new and gigantic field of scientific achievement. Not only was a single person to be recorded in every detail, good bad or indifferent, but views and scenes with 'built-in' perspective and complicated toning achieved such results that, for a period, the day of the artist was considered to be finished.

At that time the photographer sought to emulate portraits, still life and scenes such as had taken hours and even months in the hands of the true artist. Eventually the aims widened with the wish to catch the fleeting moments of history, and all possible aspects of life were recorded. Thus today a rich field of original material is available for the researcher who wishes to illustrate his special subject. The life of the soldier, whose place in history, in ceremonial and sojourns in all quarters of the globe makes a ready and rewarding subject to be tackled, is recorded in this book. The period covered here ranges from the first days of photography up to the wars of the early twentieth-century – in fact, from the formal days of mid-Victorian era to the more liberal reign of King Edward VII.

This collection of early photographs, many rare and all graphic in their story, has been divided into five groups; not too easy a task when one considers the many methods of photographing and the varying aims of the early photographers, some of whom insisted that they were to be called artists. Thus, five separate themes have been chosen in order to give the reader a comprehensive coverage of the soldier's life.

In 1839 Louis J. M. Daguerre, a Frenchman, produced a latent image on a silvered copper plate which was then exposed to fumes of iodine and fixed with sodium hyposulphate producing, at last, a permanent positive image. The process was made commercial and so any person could have their image preserved on metal, but in reverse owing to the 'mirror' process. Soldiers frequently tried to avoid this false image by wearing a belt over the wrong shoulder, or holding a scabbard sword in the right hand, but the tell-tale fastening of buttons on the front of the coat often showed the female method of fastening.

The restrictions of the daguerreotype were eased when the talbotype or calotype was evolved just before the middle of the century. This process involved the use of a paper negative and a positive being taken from it resulting in the distinctive reddish or purplish-brown print, somewhat similar to a 'sun-print'. Fox Talbot had a patent on the paper negative process which he jealously guarded and so restricted in England the free growth of photography. However, abroad many experiments took place and eventually the blockage was overcome. Thus many British amateurs in many parts of the Empire produced calotypes which included soldiers; R. Adamson and O. Hill being well known in Scotland and J. MacCosh being less known in Burma and India. Full length figures and detailed scenes were now common, with the ubiquitous soldier being shown in his military setting.

The calotype had artistic gradations and good tones but lacked the finer details. The introduction of the collodion process in 1851 which employed glass negative plates may have been awkward and cumbersome but once again further possibilities of definition opened up. This was the process employed by Roger Fenton in the Crimean War and which achieved effects hardly rivalled by the advanced techniques of today.

The aims of the early photographers were not entirely commercial. Many amateurs took up the new scientific processes as an extension of the art world to which they had been trained. Composition, light and shade and other elements of the painter's craft were stiven for and may be recognised in the photographs of Fenton and Robertson. Printers and publishers did recognise the commercial possibilities of the new invention and soon commissioned work for reproduction.

The Crimean War was an obvious sounding board for the new craft. Newspaper reportage was now developing and so the illustration side was to be improved even though the hinderance of rough campaigning and cumbersome apparatus had to be overcome. Roger Fenton is best known for his coverage of this Russian war, although others were involved. His work is the earliest war photography still existing. Fenton was a founder member of the Royal Photographic Society of Great Britain, the oldest surviving photographic society in the world today. He originally worked with the calotype but went on to the glass plate in the battlefield.

He sailed in February 1855 on the 'Hecla' to the Crimean Peninsula taking with him two assistants, Marcus Sparling, who already had a knowledge of cameras, to act as a driver and 'William' who was cook and handyman. Actually all helped with the complicated photographic preparations and processes. They took with them a travelling darkroom, converted from a wine-merchant's wagon which also served as sleeping-quarters and a kitchen. Out of the 360 photographs which he made in the four months' sojourn in the battle area only a few are shown in this work but their artistic quality makes them outstanding. His ease of manner and acquaintance with Royalty gave him the *entrée* to the tents of high-ranking officers and personalities, most of whom he photographed. He easily gained co-operation when posing groups which although contrived had the air of being natural. On his return to the United Kingdom the best of his work appeared for the public in several portfolios – 50 views of scenery and camps, 60 incidents of camp life, 30 in the Historical Portrait Gallery, plus three panoramas, the whole selling at a slightly reduced price of £63. Expensive though it may have seemed in those days, that investment in contemporary photographs would bring handsome profits today.

Her Majesty Queen Victoria, a photographer in her own right, was impressed with the possibilities of recording the war. She commissioned Joseph Cundall and R. Howlett to photograph the veterans as they returned from the 'Seat of the War in the East'. Some twenty-six of these photographs were selected for a published work which was called 'Crimean Heroes', but many more were included in the Royal Collection still preserved at Windsor. These include men of the Household Cavalry, the Rifle Brigade, the Marines and various infantrymen.

Photographers like Robertson and Beato now moved from the Crimean front to the sub-continent of India to record the Great Mutiny and other military activities. From now onwards most campaigns were recorded with a clarity and detail as had not been thought possible previously. In India the atmospheric conditions and the teeming multitudes encouraged prolific photography on a commercial basis, so much so that local native photographers entered the field. Fighting on the frontiers and animal hunts when the warrior was not engaged against two-legged opponents provided exotic coverage which Europeans brought home in large leather bound albums. It may be that the women folk preferred the recording of their many servants and the lavish balls and functions which relieved so much of the tedium of their exile.

It is not often realised that the War Office attempted to record the Crimean War even before Roger Fenton arrived there. In June 1854 Richard Nicklin, a civilian photographer, was employed by the War Office with two non-commissioned officers from the Royal Sappers and Miners to visit the Black Sea area. Unfortunately, their ship was lost in a hurricane in the following November. No record remains as to what they may have produced.

Following this disaster two young ensigns, Brandon and Dawson of the 77th Foot, took a crash course of photography before they went to the Crimea in the spring of 1855. Whatever they produced was preserved in the War Office but it was noted as deteriorating and today no evidence is available of their work in the campaign.

Another attempt was made by the War Office to give photography an official status and in March 1856 four non-commissioned officers on the Royal Engineers Establishment at Chatham were trained in the art of photography and thus began a special section for that subject. At the time of the war in Abyssinia it was decided to send men of No. 10 Company Royal Engineers under Major Pritchard to that part of Africa for the purpose of producing maps and plans by photographic processes. The portable field equipment was also used to record the countryside and prominent Ethiopians as well as troops.

Although the practical use of map-making by photography and photo-

5 Drummer boy writing home to Mother after the victory at Colesberg, South Africa, 1900

lithographic process was encouraged by the authorities, original photographs still survive to show that the results of gunfire, the creation of fieldworks and buildings were kept for reference purposes. A few prints exist to show that illustrations of men's equipment as well as that of horses were made as a guide to regulations. But these relics stamped with 'Photo. Estab. War Office' are rare and were no doubt at the time considered by some to be unnecessary fripperies.

The wars in Egypt and the Sudan were recorded by private photographers as well as newspaper representatives. The later South African or Boer War broke new ground as the coverage was not only by still camera but by the newly-emerging movie or cine-camera.

Apart from the news value of wars, the British Army at home in Victorian times had a popularity which was reflected in the many military periodicals and other illustrated publications. The Queen and her Army were evocative symbols in the days of the rich and expanding empire, the benefits of which were being appreciated in these islands. The fortnightly publication of the 'Navy and Army Illustrated' covered all facets of the soldier's life and reproductions from the studio of Gregory and Company may be seen herein. Weeklies like 'Under the Union Jack' and the 'Black and White Budget' provided coverage of the South African war but frequently the quality and definition was poor. This is where the popular stereoscopic photographs excelled. The advance of photography into the process of gelatine film, though it may have been quicker and cheaper, brought a lowering of standards in the final result and one regrets the detail and clarity of the large glass negative now gradually losing popularity.

Now on the personal front even the poorest soldier could be reproduced full length by a daguerreotype and later by the carte-de-visite photograph or tintype by local and itinerant photographers. The introduction of the personal, rather than the public, camera allowed almost anyone to try their hand and so in many cases the photographs from film are the poorest record, frequently out of focus. However much good survives.

The rich mines of mainly unpublished military material are spread throughout the United Kingdom. One of the earliest to be collected is that begun by Queen Victoria in the Royal Collection at Windsor. Not only did the Queen interest herself in the subject but she asked others to participate – the recording of the returned Crimean veterans already having been mentioned. Other and later albums provide graphic information on later campaigns.

The National Army Museum in Chelsea, perhaps the most modern collection, has now many thousands of original photographs plus a much larger coverage of copy and modern negative. The Scottish United Services Museum in Edinburgh specialises, of course, in the preservation of Scottish military items but does also have other negatives. Regimental museums may have ancient volumes of original photographs but frequently without reproduction facilities. The larger photographic agencies may often be able to produce rare old military photographs. Thus it will be seen that the persistence of the search to find good material has been rewarded in this volume. Also one must not overlook the joy of finding an original for one's own collection, several of which appear here.

THE ARMY AT HOME

6   Inspecting a recruit, 1897, at the Guards' depot at Caterham. The regiment is the Coldstream Guards. The civilian is presumably the medical officer in mufti

7   The new recruit, 1897. The sergeant's remarks on this occasion can be well imagined.
Both are wearing the white drill jackets and serving in the Coldstream Guards

8 The regimental sergeant major with two sentries, 1898. The lion on the collars denotes the King's Own Royal Lancaster Regiment. The rank badge of a crown was later altered to the royal coat of arms. Note the pad on the left shoulder to protect the red tunic from the rifle

9 Guard room at the Cavalry Barracks Aldershot, 1897. The gong was struck every hour to denote the time. A corporal of the 3rd King's Hussars is performing this duty. The men are wearing dismounted full dress. The sergeant on the right is wearing the Khedives Star Egypt, 1882 Campaign

10 (overleaf) Royal Artillery at Leith Fort, 1846. The gentlemen are Major Wright, Major Crawford, Captain St George and Captain Brettingham. The officer on the extreme right is wearing full dress except for the headdress, belts and sabretache

11 Royal engineer officers examining balloon equipment *c*. 1896. Observation balloons had been used in the American Civil War and were beginning to interest the War Department to direct artillery fire

12   92nd Gordon Highlanders, April 1846. Sergeant reading the orders of the day

13 Royal Welsh Fusiliers, 1890. The drum major and the regimental goat with the goat major. The goat mascot dates before 1777 and since 1844 has been selected from the royal herd. Within the regiment the goat is not referred to as a mascot

14 Cyclists at Bay', 1898. Awaiting an attack by the cavalry on manoeuvres. In the centre stands the officer with a bugle boy at his side

15   Life Guards in full dress off to the Royal Military Tournament 1910 by char-à-bancs

16 Drum horses of the 17th Duke of Cambridge's own Lancers, 1890. The horse was reputed to be 20 years old at this time. The drum banners carry the regimental battle honours and are embroidered in gold wire

17 A trooper of the 2nd Life Guards polishing his breastplate, with advice from his two friends. In those days the front and back plates were not plated and required much polishing, *c.* 1890

20 (*opposite*) A soldiers kit an
how it should be laid out for
inspection. A Seaforth
Highlander, *c.* 1890. He is
wearing the white drill jacket
and tartan trews

18 A wounded or sick soldier
at Netley Hospital with his
mother *c.* 1900. He is wearing
the hospital uniform which was
much the same as that used in
the Crimea War

19 'Two's company'. Epping
Forest on a Sunday afternoon,
c. 1900. The lucky soldier is
from the Royal Engineers

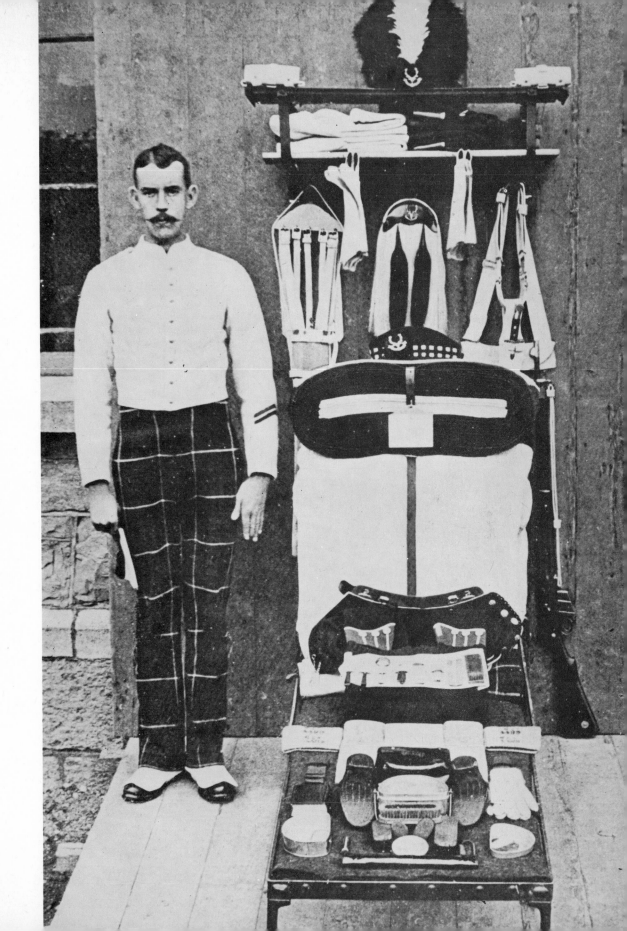

22 Bootmaker of the 3rd Kings Own Hussars, 1899. Every
regiment repaired its own boots

Three Royal Horse Artillery officers, 1867. Captains
liot and Murray and Lieutenant Yorke. The uniform
anged little until the end of full dress, note the rank worn
the collars and the more elaborate sleeves of the captains

23 (*top left*) Bandmaster of the 1st Royal Dragoons, 1902. The helmet plume is white for the band and he wears a gold embroidered lyre on his right arm

24 (*above*) Orderly men of the Irish Guards leaving the cook house with food. The meal was consumed in their own barrack room, 1903

25 (*left*) A rough rider corporal of the 17th Lancers shows how the unfortunate horse would be used as shelter in open country, 1895

26 Royal Horse Artillery, 1900. The gun is unlimbered with the horses at the rear

27 A group of sergeants at cards, 1902. A mess waiter stands at the left. This is a cavalry regiment, possibly at Canterbury

28 Troopers of the 3rd Kings Own Hussars at stable duty, 189

29 Farrier quartermaster sergeant instructing his men which would include eight sergeant farriers and four shoeing smiths. These are all under the command of the regimental veterinary surgeon, 1899

30 Wounded or sick soldier at Netley Hospital, 1901

31 Irish Guards cleaning their kit for inspection, 1903. They are wearing the Broderick cap issued between 1900 and 1905

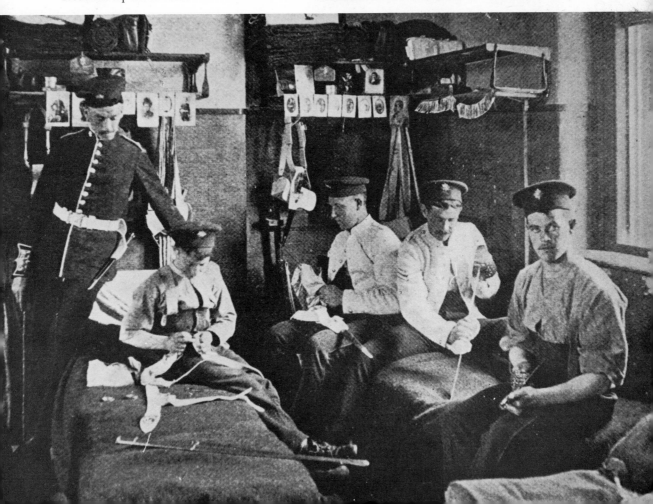

32   Soldiers at Coal Fatigue nicknamed, 'regimental sports', 1898

33   Display of goods available at the Royal Horse Guards' canteen during the cavalry manoeuvres of 1890. The boxes of this affluent regiment are marked 'Harrods'

34 Sargeant Patterson and the staff of the Aldershot Gymnasium rehearsing for the 1895 Royal Military Tournament

35 (*overleaf*) 2nd Life Guards at dinner, 1894. Note the soldier in the centre finishing off the stew

36 Soldiers of the 11th Prince Albert's Own Hussars bed-filling, 1897. The men are wearing side caps and fatigues

37 A smart turn out of the guard, formed by the 6th Dragoon Guards (Carabiniers). The helmet plume is white, the tunics blue with white facings. On dismounted guard duty the men carried carbines, *c.* 1890

38 Band of the 1st Battalion Grenadier Guards, 1874. Note the extreme youth of the drummer boys. On the left stands the drum major. Wearing the white apron is the bass drummer, his medals include those for the Crimea

39 Royal Horse Guards' 'drag', *c.* 1870. This was used at race meetings and other sporting occasions. The door is painted with the regimental crest

40 Camp guard of the Seaforth Highlanders, 1896. The man standing next to the sergeant on the left is a bugler.

41 Grenadier Guards non-commissioned officers, *c.* 1870. Seated on the ground is the regimental sergeant major. An officer stands on the steps

42 Sergeants' Mess of the Irish Guards, 1903. The fittings are quite luxurious when compared with the barrack room

43 Barrack Room, 1900. The beds are folded away in daytime. The walls are heavily plastered with pin-ups

44 Tailors of the Irish Guards altering and repairing uniforms, *c.* 1905. The hat was no doubt brought back from South Africa

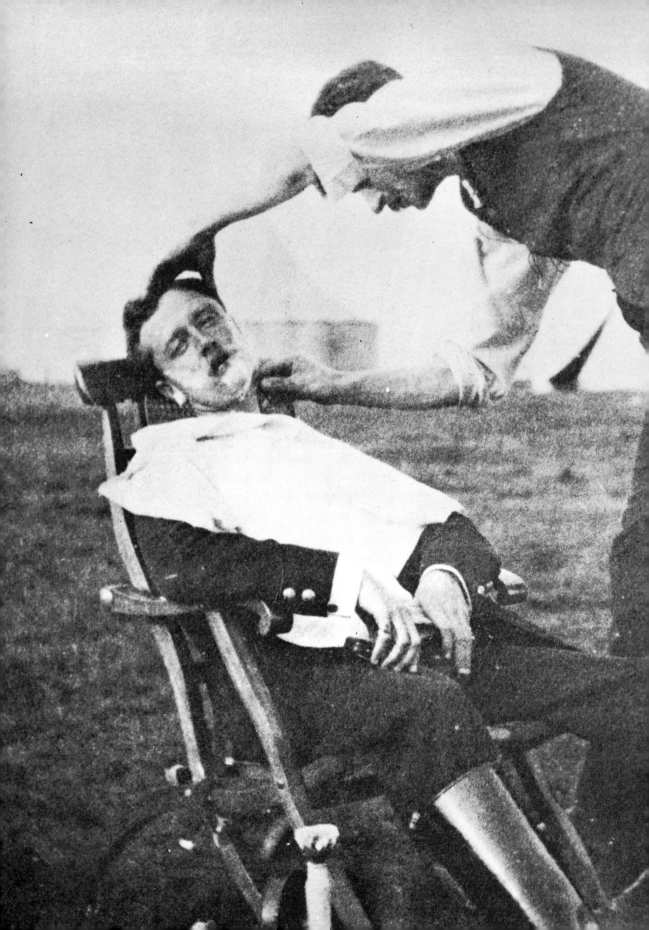

46 Drawing water at camp for cooking when under canvas, *c.* 1896

45 Colonel's early morning shave. Cavalry manoeuvres, *c.* 1890.

47 (*above*) 2nd Life Guards'
cookhouse at Lockinge, 1894

48 (*left*) 1st Life Guards
corporal majors, 1861. They are
wearing the scarlet stable jacket
with the forage cap

49 (*right*) Bear mascot of the
17th Lancers, *c.* 1898

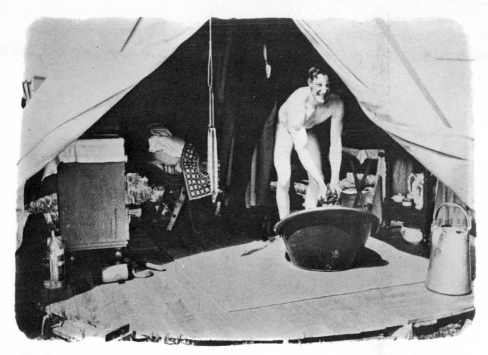

50 Under canvas bathing.

51 'The British Square', 1861. Formed by the 1st Battalion Grenadier Guards. H.R.H. The Prince of Wales in command at The Curragh, Ireland

52   Band of the 7th Queen's Own Hussars, *c.* 1890. The kettledrum banners are displayed at the front. The band sergeant stands on the extreme left, baton in hand

53 Saddlers of the 17th Lancers, 1896. On the right a man is repairing an officer's shabraque. In the foreground can be seen a pair of pistol holsters

PERSONALITIES

54   Edward Prince of Wales, 1859, as colonel on the staff

56 (*above*) Prince Albert, *c*. 1850, in the uniform of a field marshal. The prince was also colonel of the Rifle Brigade

57 (*above right*) George, Duke of York, later George V, with his ADC the Hon. Derek Keppel at Osborne, 1897. The duke wears the uniform of the Isle of Wight Rifles

58 (*right*) Edward VII in the uniform of a field marshal with his two sons Albert Victor and George, who on the death of his elder brother became heir to the throne

55 (*opposite*) Albert Victor Duke of Clarence, 1864–92. Eldest son of Edward VII. in the uniform of the 10th Prince of Wales' Own Hussars

59 H.R.H. George, Duke of Cambridge. Commander-in-chief of the
British army from 1856 to 1895

60 The Prince Imperial, son of Napoleon III, in the uniform of the Royal Artillery. He was killed in the Zulu War of 1879

61 Field Marshal Lord Kitchener, 1902. On his appointment as commander-in-chief India. He then held the rank of General and was appointed field marshal in 1909

63 (*opposite*) General Charles George Gordon, *c.* 1860. Fought in the Crimea and China, subsequently killed at Khartoum in 1885. He is wearing the uniform of the Royal Engineers

62 The Earl of Lucan, 1865. Colonel of the Life Guards. Commanded the cavalry in the Crimea

64 Field Marshal Garnet Wolseley, *c.* 1870. Served in the Burma War 1853, Crimea, Indian Mutiny, Canada and the Ashanti War. Field marshal in 1894 and following year commander-in-chief

65 Lieutenant-Colonel Sam Browne v.c., *c.* 1858. Lost his arm and gained his v.c. in the Indian Mutiny. Despite the loss he rose to the rank of general. He invented the Sam Browne belt adopted by practically every army of the world

66 Major-General Baden Powell, 1903. He won great popularity for his defence of Mafeking in the Boer War and was appointed Inspector-General of Cavalry in 1903

67 General Sir Redvers Buller with the 17th Lancers, 1888, when acting as quartermaster-general. He was superseded by Lord Roberts in South Africa after several severe reverses.

68 Florence Nightingale, 1820–1910. Volunteered for service in the Crimea and sailed with 34 nurses in 1854. Her self sacrificing services to the wounded made her famous throughout Europe

69 The resplendent Hugh 5th Earl of Londsdale at the Delhi Durbar, 1903. He is wearing the uniform of the Westmorland and Cumberland Yeomanry of which he was colonel

70 Six Indian Mutiny v.cs, 1910. Left to right, Lieutenant-General Sir James Hills-John, Major-General Luke O'Connor, Field Marshal Sir Evelyn Wood, Field Marshal Rt. Hon. Earl Roberts, Field Marshal Sir George White, Colonel Sir Edward Thackeray, taken at the Royal Hospital, Chelsea

THE CRIMEA

71 Colonel Lord George Paget, 4th Light Dragoons, on his charger, with Lieutenant-Colonel John Douglas 11th Prince Albert's Own Hussars, 1854

72 (*overleaf*) Camp of the 4th Royal Irish Dragoon Guards. The officer in the centre is typical of the type of dress worn in this campaign, 1855

74 Sergeant-Major Edwards, Scots Fusilier Guards. He wears the double-breasted tunic withdrawn, 1856. His badge of rank is the royal coat of arms superimposed on four chevrons

3 Tea in the Crimea, 1855. The officer on the left wears
athered overalls. A form of thermos flask appears to be
 use

75 Royal Sappers and Miners, Colour-Sergeant Stanton, Colour Sergeant Knight and Private Bruce wearing the new single-breasted tunic of 1857

76   17th Lancers, 1856. Survivors of the Light Brigade.
They are from left to right Corporal Thomas Smith, A troop;
Corporal William Dimmock, F troop; Private William
Pearson, A troop and Corporal Thomas Foster, A troop

77   Colour Sergeant of the 78th Highlanders. He is wearing
the short-lived double-breasted doublet of 1856. The
diamond shaped buttons were peculiar to Highland
regiments

78   Captain Henry and Mrs Duberly in the Light Cavalry camp before Sevastapol, 1855. The
captain was Paymaster to the 8th Kings Royal Irish Hussars

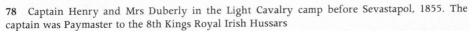

79   (*overleaf*) Lieutenant-General Sir George Brown seated in the centre with his staff, 1855.
Behind the general stands an elderly soldier, his orderly or servant

80 5th The Princess Charlotte of Wales' Regiment of Dragoon Guards, 1855. Part of the Heavy Brigade. The full dress helmet was worn minus the plume

81 British officers with a French *cantinière*, 1855. The officers look jovial, the girl apprehensive. They wear the shell jacket with undress caps

82 Soldiers and an officer in winter fur coats called 'bunnies' sent out from England, 1855

83 Cornet Watkins 11th Prince Albert's Own Hussars. This regiment was part of the Light Brigade. The officer is in review order except without the shabraque, 1854

84   Lieutenant-Colonel Thomas Shadforth and his officers of the 57th West Middlesex Regiment, 1854

85 Officers of the 42nd Royal Highlanders, 1855. The officer on the left is wearing full dress except for the headdress. All are carrying highland swords

86 (*above left*) A pioneer and two guardsmen of the Grenadier Guards, 1856. This photograph shows very well the equipment carried by the men. The pioneer is wearing an apron

87 (*above*) Trumpeter George Gritton 11th Battalion and trumpeter W. Long 12th Battalion Royal Artillery, 1854, with Russian trophy. Both are wearing Crimea medals but have not been issued with the new tunics

88 (*left*) Rifleman of the Rifle Brigade wearing the pre-1856 coatee complete with epaulettes. This is the uniform worn when the regiment left for the Crimea. The shako was called the 'Albert' having been designed by Prince Albert

89 (*opposite*) 'Valley of the Shadow of Death'.

90 Lieutenant-Colonel Hallewell receives a drink from his servant after a day's work, 1854

91 Three shockingly wounded soldiers from the Crimea who were visited by the Queen at Chatham on their return

92 Two wounded soldiers holding the shot that injured them. Both with facial wounds, 1855

THE ARMY IN INDIA

93 Nusaree Battalion. Gurkhas with their commanding officer Alexander Bagot, 1857. The Gurkhas remained our allies during the Indian Mutiny. The sitting figure with his back to the camera clearly shows the *kukri*

94　(*top left*) Sergeant of Horse Artillery, *c.* 1848, by John MaCosh. The earliest military photographer in India, the sergeant wears an oilskin cover to his cap

95　(*left*) Major-General Sir Hope Grant, 1857. Commanded the cavalry at the Siege of Delhi, taking part in the relief of Cawnpore and the retaking of Lucknow

96 Lieutenant C. H. Meecham and Assistant Surgeon T. Anderson. The laxity in dress during the arduous Mutiny campaign clearly shows: loose cloths, a sun helmet and weapons stuffed into cummerbunds

97 Major Henry Kavanagh v.c. who disguised himself as a native and slipped out of besieged Lucknow to reach Sir Colin Campbell with vital information. In the photograph he is seated in the centre of a group of 1st European Bengal Fusiliers. The officer wearing the shako and white linen trousers is Captain Trevor Wheeler. Wearing a peaked cap seated next to Kavanagh is Ensign Henry Halford. Standing in the doorway is Lieutenant Montagu Hall, an engineer under General Havelock. Seated in the doorway is Lieutenant Wynyard Warner. The officer in a slouch hat, belt over the left shoulder is Captain Hamilton Maxwell, half brother to Lord Roberts

98 Part of the barracks at Cawnpore held by General Wheeler showing the effects of bombardment, 1858

99 Heavy artillery moved by elephants, 1858

100 Officers of the Nizam of Hyderabad's bodyguard, 1890. The venerable officer in the centre is the Commandant Amir Ul Umrah – the title was hereditary

101 The son of the regimental adjutant with soldiers of a Baluchi regiment, 1903

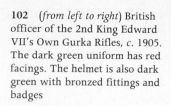

102 (*from left to right*) British officer of the 2nd King Edward VII's Own Gurka Rifles, *c.* 1905. The dark green uniform has red facings. The helmet is also dark green with bronzed fittings and badges

103 A Havildar of the 11th Bengal Native Infantry, 1887. This was a Rajput regiment

104 A Duffadar of the 11th Bengal Lancers, 1886. He was a Jat Sikh heavily armed with lance, sword and carbine. Duffadar is the rank of sergeant

105 Rifleman of the 3rd Gurkha Rifles, 1886. Uniform was dark green with black facings

106 (*opposite*) British officer 11th Prince of Wales' Own Lancers. This is one of the m elaborate of Indian uniforms The collar, front, skirts and shoulders are embroidered in gold. The crest of the Prince Wales can be seen on the po belt. The sword was also peculiar to the regiment and similar to a general officers, *c.* 1890

107   13th Duke of Connaught's regiment of Bengal Lancers, *c.* 1890. On the left a duffadar, in the centre an Indian officer and on the right a trooper or sowar

109   Members of Lord Curzon's staff being carried ashore at Aden, 1903

108 Bombay Cavalry on camels used in the desert areas of the Scinde by the 5th Bombay Cavalry (Scinde Horse), *c.* 1890

110   Punjab Infantry, *c.* 1857. A photograph of Mutiny-raised Indian soldiers. Two Indian officers stand at the back

111 Major Sir Louis Cavagnari with Amir Yakub Khan, 1879. Four months later Cavagnari was murdered and the Afghan War began

112   5th Pujab Infantry in position at Sherpur outside Kabul, December 1879. Afghan Campaign

113 Lieutenant-Colonel Hamley of the 50th Regiment with his family and servants, *c.* 1891

114 Regimental ball of the Royal Irish Fusiliers, *c.* 1910, at Belgaum. The regimental motto above the door is the battle cry of the regiment 'clear the way'

115 A Lucknow wedding, *c.* 1890. The bridegroom is from the 3rd Gurkha Rifles. On the left stands an officer of possibly the 6th King Edward's 12th Bengal Cavalry. On the right an officer on the Staff

116 (*overleaf*) Mr McNab's luncheon party, *c.* 1880. Several young ladies at lunch with Indian Army officers

117   Interior of a barrack room 44th Regiment, 1875. The high rooms are painted white. The room has been laid out for an inspection

118   Interior of the officers' mess. 44th Regiment, 1875. The two decanters of port have reached the right hand side

119   Interior of native Indian troops barrack room, c. 1880. Equipment of beds are laid out similar to those of the British troops

120 British and Indian horsemen playing polo, *c.* 1910. One of the oldest of games (brought from Persia) and very popular with cavalry and infantry regiments

121 A British square, India, *c.* 1870. Field officers' horses are being held on the left side. The regimental colours can be seen in the centre. The casualties from such a close formation can be imagined

122 Graves of British soldiers, Chitral Campaign, 1895. At Haram Kotal

123 Soldiers in action at Peiwar Kotah. Afghan War, 1879. They are advancing against entrenched Afghan positions

124 The King's Own Scottish Borderers in action at the Arhanga Pass, Tirah Campaign, 1897. All the men are wearing tartan trews. A machine gun is in action on the left

125 The Dorset Regiment attacking the Sampaga Pass. Tirah Campaign, 1897. The soldier on the left appears to be amused by something?

126   The Gordon Highlanders advancing up the Heights of Dargai. Tirah Campaign, 1897

127 1st Battalion Royal West Kent Regiment resting at Kingurgulli, North West Frontier, 1898. The two soldiers in the front have acquired Indian tulwars. An officer stands behind them. On the right a soldier is having his hair cut

128 Sighting a gun at Lucknow, 1857. Captain F. C. Maude, V.C. with his Battery at Letchmenteera. Maude's Battery was the only Royal Artillery at Lucknow. Two others were East India Company Batteries

129 A group of loyal sepoys, Indian Mutiny, 1857. The figure second from the left is an Indian officer

130 Royal Horse Artillery at Lucknow, 1858, Indian Mutiny. Their forage caps are swathed in white pugarees. The guns and limbers can be seen under the trees

131   Removal of a dead Tibetan, 1904. This war was fought due to the hostile reception accorded
to a trade mission sent by the Government of India

AFRICA

132 Captain Charles Speedy, Chief Intelligence Officer on Napier's Staff, Abyssinian War, 1868. A colourful character over 6 ft 5 inches tall, he had fought for the Emperor of Abyssinia in 1860 and had been made a General, fought in New Zealand and then returned to Africa upon the offer of Sir Robert Napier. He disappeared after the war; his fate remains unknown. The photograph shows him dressed as an Abyssinian General

133 Isandhlwana. A sentry guards the wrecked wagon park on May 21, 1879 while the Cavalry searches the battle-field beyond

134 Major-General Lord Chelmsford. General command-ing the forces in South Africa during the Zulu War, 1879 and defeated at Isandhlwana

135 (*right*) Lieutenant John Rouse Merriott Chard, v.c. wearing his medal with a group of fellow Royal Engineer officers in camp towards the Campaign. His defence of Rorke's Drift with Lieutenant Bromhead of the 24th Foot won himself and his companions eleven v.c.'s; the largest number ever awarded for one action, most of which had been a desperate hand to hand struggle lasting ten hours

136 Mounted Infantry Camel Regiment, 1885, formed for the Sudan Campaign. The men are carrying Martini Henry rifles

137 (*below*) View of the camp at Handouk, Sudan, 1885. Cavalry lines on the left. In the centre are camels. A zareba of thorns encloses the whole encampment

138 10th Prince of Wales' Own Hussars' officer scouting, 1885. He is wearing his full dress pouch belt over his shoulder and blue overalls with the double stripes; his tunic and helmet are khaki

139 Battle of Atbara, 1898 Sudan Campaign. British troops in square formation awaiting the attack

140 Roll call of the Warwickshire Regiment after the Battle of Atbara, 1898

141　Egyptian troops leaving the battlefield of Atbara, 1898

142　Egyptian troops bury the Dervish dead after the Battle of Atbara, 1898

143 Ten minutes before the Battle of Omdurman, 1898. British troops at ease

144 Troops firing at the Dervishes, machine gun on the left. Battle of Omdurman, 1898

145   A lull in the Battle. The paper in which the cartridges are wrapped litter the ground. Omdurman, 1898

146   MacDonald's Brigade in action, the Dervishes can be seen firing at the top of the photograph. Omdurman, 1898

147   (*overleaf*) General Gateacre calling 'ceasefire' after the Battle of Omdurman, 1898

148   Spion Kop disaster in the Boer War, 1900, the most costly battle of General Buller's Campaign. The trench is filled with British dead

149   After the Battle of Spion Kop, medical orderlies search the heaped bodies for the living, 1900

150   British scouts firing at a Boer Patrol near Colesburg, 1900

151 Royal Munster Fusiliers lining the trenches on a Boer alarm, Honey Nest Kloof, 1901

152   The last drop. A scene on the battlefield of Dordrecht, South Africa

153 Lydite shell bursting in front of a Boer gun emplacement. Much of the Boer artillery was German in origin, mostly Krupp pieces

154 The soldier's farewell; a typical tear jerker of the
period, *c.* 1900